# CONFIRMATION COOK BOOK

A compendium of outlines
for a flexible training course
in the Christian Faith

*compiled by*

David Manship,
Margaret Hayes, Philip Johnson,
Michael Joint and Ruth Wild

*Foreword by the Bishop of Winchester*

MOWBRAY
LONDON & OXFORD

Copyright © David Manship, 1980

ISBN 0 264 66029 3

First published in 1980 by A. R. Mowbray & Co. Ltd.,
Saint Thomas House, Becket Street,
Oxford, OX1 1SJ
**Reprinted 1982**

Typeset by Input Typesetting Ltd and
Printed in Great Britain by Sawtells of Sherborne Ltd

*No part of this book may be reproduced or transmitted
in any form or by any means, electronic or
mechanical, including photocopying, recording
or by any information storage and retrieval
system, without permission in writing from the Publisher.*

# CONTENTS

| | | |
|---|---|---|
| *Foreword by the Bishop of Winchester* | | *page* 5 |
| *Introduction* | | 7 |
| 1 | FOOD FOR THOUGHT – about the task in hand | 9 |
| 2 | FEEDING THE FAMILY – thoughts on a style of training | 12 |
| 3 | THOUGHT FOR FOOD – towards a balanced diet | 16 |
| 4 | DISHES TO SERVE – for your Confirmation group | 20 |
| | MYSELF | 21 |
| | FELLOWSHIP | 24 |
| | JESUS | 28 |
| | MAN AND GOD | 31 |
| | FAITH | 36 |
| | SACRAMENTS | 39 |
| | DISCIPLESHIP | 43 |
| 5 | OUTLINING A DIET – a report from St Agnes' | 46 |

# FOREWORD
# BY THE BISHOP OF WINCHESTER

If you haven't put the plug in you won't fill your bath, not even by turning on the taps to full pressure. Neither can we deal with the problem of diminishing numbers in our Church by organising special missions and drives. The run-away wastage will go on until we attend to the places where the leaks are.

The biggest of all the leaks is the annual loss of most of those who have recently been confirmed. If they could be committed for more than two years and stay with the Church when they grow older and get married we would have far younger congregations and a growing Church. So, attending to their needs is worth more than all our other efforts, good as they are.

Attending to them means finding ways of holding their interest and giving them real responsibilities *after* they have been confirmed. But equally important is the instruction and preparation they receive *before* confirmation. I am dismayed by the old-fashioned courses I so frequently find being used by those who do this training in the parishes, and even more appalled by those parishes that follow no printed syllabus at all. So I welcome this manual which our own Diocesan Education Team has prepared for those who undertake to teach confirmation candidates.

Use the 'Cook Book'. Like a collection of good recipes, it ought to be adhered to quite strictly at first. But, as you gain more experience of these methods of 'cooking', you can experiment and adapt so as to set your own mark on the results. The ingredients we have to hand are as good as they have ever been. I am full of hope whenever I chat with confirmation candidates, young or old. They deserve the best we can give them. So again, please pay close attention to this book.

*John Winton*

# INTRODUCTION

It is some years now since the Report of the Commission on Christian Initiation (the Ely Report) was published and debated in the General Synod.

Some of its detailed recommendations were not accepted, including the suggestion that young people should be admitted to Holy Communion early, before making their adult commitment to a Christian way of life and faith.

This decision has tended to obscure the importance of the Report's main thrust towards the need to surround a young person with an experience of continuous training throughout childhood and early adulthood, and of its insistence that this experience should be matched to the needs and capacity of young people as they grow. This means that we must pay more attention to the quality of the training offered to young people and adults, both before and after their Confirmation.

This compendium of suggestions from which group leaders can make their own selection is one attempt to meet this need.

We have resisted the temptation to produce a set piece. This would have been easier, but could not possibly have suited the great variety of circumstances, and could have been seriously misleading. We offer instead our 'Confirmation Cook Book' out of which it should be possible to produce a well-balanced diet, and a number of nourishing and palatable dishes to suit the needs of most of those who present themselves for Confirmation, at whatever age.

In doing so, however, we wish to emphasise that no course in itself can provide the nourishment that new Christians require. Real nourishment comes only from a nourishing community.

*Winchester Diocesan Education Team – 1979*
*David Manship*
*Margaret Hayes*
*Philip Johnson*
*Michael Joint*
*Ruth Wild*

# 1 FOOD FOR THOUGHT
*–about the task in hand*

## VARIETY

Those who come forward for Confirmation vary enormously in age and background, in attitude and experience, in how able or committed they are, in what motivates them, and in the things they expect. Buildings, timetables, leadership, local tradition and opportunities will also vary. Because of this it is essential that those responsible for the training recognise, and make the most of, local circumstances. The important thing is to know all the candidates by name (in the Biblical sense of 'in their true nature'), to reach out to each one as a person, and to make that the starting point.

## SPECIAL OPPORTUNITY

From cradle to grave there are many opportunities at home, school, Church, Sunday School, or through the media, to learn about religion and faith, but Confirmation and the training associated with it have special opportunities and a special *raison de'être*. Some interpret it as a decisive step towards another level of discipleship. For some it is a spiritual equivalent to puberty when new levels of awareness and new powers are awakened. It may be interpreted by others as a particularly critical moment in a re-education process, an upward spiral of learning in which childish ideas or misconceptions are unlearned and replaced by something more mature and first-hand. Others again see it as a rite of passage from childhood to adulthood which says something about moving into a new set of relationships – being received by, belonging and being committed to, an adult believing community. This last has implications for the community as well as for the candidate.

Whatever picture you choose, no-one can guarantee that the particular candidates are actually experiencing at the precise moment of their training such new levels of religious awareness. We trust that everyone will have a springtime – a period of personal development – but for some it will have happened beforehand, and for others it may come a lot later, or not at all. Training can, however, be designed to reflect or promote this new growth. It will be seen as induction as well as education, a beginning rather than an end, a vision shared rather than the presentation of the last word. There is the temptation to deliver final answers in pre-packaged form, and the fear of leaving out something vital, which lead to the disastrous paths of instant communication and of attempting too much: 'We will do God this week and Jesus next.' The difficult challenge is not to find out what you can put into the course, but to learn how much you can bear to leave out with a good conscience.

## SHARED LEADERSHIP

Traditionally it was always the vicar or his assistant who prepared the candidates for Confirmation, and doubtless there are places where this will still be thought to be the best practice. There are, however, many advantages in asking a group of lay people to share in this. First it accords with the ideal of shared ministry, and gives lay people the opportunity for real responsibility. Secondly, a group of people can between them offer more to the candidates than can one individual – more stimulus, more variety, more personalities to meet. Thirdly, the need for the adult worshipping community to welcome its new members into fellowship is already beginning to be met in the fellowship enjoyed by leaders and candidates. Fourthly, there is within the group of leaders the opportunity of sharing among themselves different leadership roles – some to act as hosts, some to lead a group, some to attend to administration, some to put candidates in touch with adult worshippers, some to give their expert knowledge. The vicar's contribution may be in this last category, or another may be best for his talents: in any case his responsibility is to oversee the enterprise.

## THE ADULT COMMUNITY

As hinted above, Confirmation preparation is as much to do with preparing the adult community to receive and care for its new members, as it is to do with preparing candidates to enter the adult community.

There are various ways of working towards this difficult objective. Many members of the congregation who fight shy of leading a group could nevertheless be involved by being asked to invite the candidates to their homes, making them welcome, and answering their questions. House groups might open their membership temporarily or permanently to candidates, and examine the possibility of house communions. Adults who are already confirmed might share in the training as a refresher course.

Posts of responsibility in the adult community (community service, sidesmen, street wardens, etc) might be made ready and waiting for the candidates to fill. The sincerity, quality and scope of the worship will have an effect on the new members: its form might need to be modified, and opportunities found for them not only to serve but to take a growing share in leadership.

# 2 FEEDING THE FAMILY
– *thoughts on a style of training*

## WAYS OF LEARNING

There is a difference between 'knowing' and 'knowing about'. Both have their place in Confirmation training.

'Knowing about' is an activity of the mind and involves learning facts and receiving information. Such knowledge may only be slightly related to the candidates' experience, but even so you can make the most of what experience there is by using methods other than straight 'telling', such as projects, research, discussions, games, to help the learners make the knowledge their own.

There is also a right *moment* for teaching *about* things; when questions are beginning to be asked, for example, or after the candidates have shared some experience and it would be helpful to give them some concepts or facts to interpret it. Sometimes, because we do not have all the time in the world, we may feel we have to take a short cut by telling candidates certain things in a concentrated way.

There is, therefore, a right use of direct teaching, but there is also a wrong use, when it is given irrespective of the candidates' ability to receive it and make use of it, when it deprives them of a deeper understanding that they might have had if they had discovered it for themselves, or when too much is given too soon. The test question which every leader should ask is not 'What am I teaching?' but 'What are they learning?'.

'Knowing', on the other hand, is more fundamental. It necessarily is personal, is interior, and implies a direct relationship. This kind of knowledge is bound to be based on the candidates' experience, and the leader must design the training with this in mind.

There are three ways of relating what is to be learned to the candidates' experience. The first helps to draw on their past, recall it, assess it and learn from it. The second provides them with an opportunity for a shared experience in the training itself (e.g. a group outing, a project). This will include the important factor of how the candidates feel about their leaders. Sometimes such an experience can be left to speak for itself (as when a good spirit of fellowship emerges), or it may be discussed and assessed (as with some of the games and exercises recommended in chapter four). The third way is to help candidates to enter vividly into other peoples' experience through the imaginative telling of stories or through drama.

But even if all these ways are used, you cannot *make* a person have an experience! We must guard against manipulation. Moreover, people are likely to experience things at different levels; they can be more or less receptive, depending on their temperament and a host of other factors. The important thing is to provide the opportunities, and to aim for the possibility of as deep a level as possible, for it is the deeper experiences, whether of fun, fellowship, challenge, compassion or wonder, that impress and make their impact.

## EXPERIENCE AND SACRAMENT

Some people attach enormous significance to the Confirmation service, and argue that because it is a sacrament in which God acts to strengthen the candidate, then that is the key moment alongside which any preparatory training or follow up is purely incidental.

Others argue that because God clearly works through people and their experience, the key thing is not the Confirmation service, which is but a moment in the total experience of the candidates, but all the training that surrounds it and the relationships that are built up.

We would wish to claim that both are important in different ways, and each is damaged by any shortcoming of the other. For us the service of Confirmation sums up and represents sacramentally all that we are trying to realise and awaken in the life and experience of the candidates and the worshipping community that is to receive them.

There are implications in this view for the candidates and their leaders. It will be wrong to build up false expectations about the significance of the service as an experience, leading perhaps to disappointment later on; for its value is not in what it feels like, but in what it stands for. It will be wrong to put the service across as a great climax – the crowning at the end of an ever-growing religious experience; for it is not an end, but a beginning. Similarly it would be wrong to *expect* that every candidate who enrols at the beginning should be committed to being Confirmed. This could result in a double evil – a candidate might go through the Confirmation conventionally because of the social pressures, or suffer a sense of failure and rejection if he did not go through with it. Far better if there is an understanding from the start that the training is open and that the decision whether to be Confirmed is not automatic and not the candidate's alone. It should be freely and carefully made at the right moment in the course of the training. The basis for the decision is whether the candidate feels that he has enough glimmerings of an 'inward and spiritual grace' – beginning, however tenderly, to grow in his own experience with promise for the future – to enable him to be associated with the 'outward and visible sign' without losing his integrity.

## MAKING IT YOUR OWN

As it is so important to help candidates make new knowledge their very own, it may be helpful to notice some ways of working to this end. The leader must provide time, space and opportunity for the following:

*Time to reflect*: an opportunity to be still and silent, to digest and come to terms with what has been going on, or with any new thoughts or ideas which have been expounded.

*Time to evaluate*: an opportunity to weigh evidence and work out the value and worth of different experiences.

*Time to affirm*: an opportunity to make a personal response – to 'say yes to', own up to, admit to oneself, rejoice in all that is true of oneself, of other people, of the world, of God.

*Time to act*: an opportunity to express what one has learned or discovered, through one of the arts, drama, community service, or worship, so offering it back to God.

## PEOPLE COME FIRST

People come first, before syllabuses and standards of knowledge. While we do not go along with those who make a false distinction between pandering to personal need and setting high and demanding standards of achievement (some people need to be challenged) nevertheless we wish to draw attention to the danger of setting an academic standard in such a way as to outlaw ignorance, and reject those unable to keep up. (Indeed there will always be individuals for whom an academic approach will be inappropriate). The better approach is to set an atmosphere in which candidates feel able to share their ignorance as well as their knowledge.

The syllabus must not be allowed to tyrannise the candidates. It is more important to abandon any syllabus for the sake of the needs of the candidates, than to get through it at all costs. Unfortunately, abandoning the syllabus can be a big threat to the leaders, who will need to ask themselves just how free they are to be flexible, and what it is that is stopping them. If leaders are free enough to enjoy the candidates in all their variety of background and ability, and to delight in exploring and receiving the ideas, hopes, fears and feelings of each one taking part, they will also incidentally cover as much of the syllabus as matters, and much more besides.

## CONTEXT COMMUNICATES

The *setting* in which people meet – the physical surroundings, the assumptions and attitudes of the leaders, their relationships with one another and with the candidates, and the way they teach and lead is an even more powerful agent of communication, for good or ill, than the subject matter. Many noble sentiments have been unconsciously denied or contradicted by the setting in which someone has tried to put them over. We have seen children harangued about their preciousness in the eyes of God while huddled forlornly in the corner of a cold and filthy backstage room in some tatty hall, amidst the broken props. We have heard the importance of love and attention extolled by a teacher whose method was 'sit down, shut up and take notes,' followed by an unceremonious dismissal on the dot of finishing time. We have heard the virtues of democracy upheld by a dominating teacher who did not let anyone take part. In all these instances, the setting and the relationships communicated unerringly while the words remained unheard or were quickly forgotten.

Of course, none of this denies the crucial importance of getting the verbal message right. We will get nowhere if the Gospel is not preached. But the Gospel is more than words; it is about the incarnate Word, and therefore is communicated in our lives as well as with our lips. *How* training is presented, then, matters as much as *what* is presented. We need to attend to the 'ambience'. Confirmation sessions conducted in a parish hall, a vicarage study, a church, a vestry, a drawing room, will all be different. Meeting in rows, in circles, in easy chairs, at desks, on the floor, will all have different effects. For our part we make no bones about favouring an approach which encourages every person to feel so accepted and understood and at home that he can truly entrust himself to the whole enterprise, and to those who are sharing it with him.

# 3 THOUGHT FOR FOOD
*– towards a balanced diet*

## THE DIET

Eating unsuitable food – too stodgy, too sweet – damages your teeth and waistline. Eating too much, too quickly, brings the risk of indigestion. The best diet is varied, enjoyable and good for you. The confirmation diet should be similarly selective. It should give variety and interest, stimulate health and growth in Christian living, and be adapted to the consumer's age and needs. We are recommending a continuing diet which is carefully chosen from a range of nourishing and essential foods.

The essentials of the diet fall into seven sections:

1. *Myself*: my identity, history and uniqueness; who I am physically, mentally, emotionally and spiritually; my potential and what makes for my wholeness . . .
2. *Fellowship*: belonging, families, groups, sharing and interdependence, community and Church . . .
3. *Jesus*: his mission, motivation and distinctiveness; good news for the poor and sinners – forgiveness and a new start; 'abba' and the 'reign of God'; his demands and his followers; his death, resurrection and exaltation; the future . . .
4. *Man and God*: man's awareness of mystery, and his response to it; religious quest and understanding; the Bible, Judaism, Christianity and other faiths; praying . . .
5. *Faith*: belief and trust, uncertainty and doubt; assent and commitment; attitudes and values . . .
6. *Sacraments*: baptism and confirmation; sin and reconciliation; eucharist . . .
7. *Discipleship*: being a Christian at home, school, work, in Church and community; life-style and vision; mission and ministry to the world; freedom and love . . .

Our categories and their contents are open to dispute. Topics could be at home in more than one section. If you think this, we hope that you will make your own connections. Again, you may think that our basic diet is eccentric, biased or wrong. While we are convinced of its balance, we hope you will feel free to adjust emphases and to remedy omissions.

## THE MEAL

This is a group-session lasting, usually, one to one and a half hours: but time is flexible. It resembles a meal because it can consist of two or three 'dishes': maybe a starter, a main course and something to finish with. Sometimes the main dish will be sufficient by itself; at other times it may be light, like a soufflé, rather than heavy and filling.

## THE DISH

The dishes from which you will devise your meals are arranged in Chapter four under the seven section-headings. There is something appropriate for every age-group and a choice of experiences – doing, listening, researching, expressing and so on. We have indicated when a dish is especially suitable as a starter, main course or finisher. We have, occasionally, suggested particular dishes which form a sequence. But, above all, we urge you to be imaginative, to experiment for yourself and to devise your own menus.

## PLANNING A DIET

You now need to decide how long the training programme (diet) is going to last: two months, a year, more – and whether the group will meet regularly (week by week for instance), or in blocks of six or eight weeks at a time (which could include a residential conference) separated by holidays.

Whatever the length of the course, you should aim to 'consume' a main dish from every section. (You need not keep to our order, though we feel that it is natural). If you are meeting only fourteen times, that may mean producing two dishes from every section. But you may consider that one main dish from a particular section is enough, and therefore choose an extra dish from elsewhere, as you think best. If your programme is going to last a year or more, you will return to each category three or four times, using new dishes or repeating old ones in a fresh way and at greater depth.

## PLANNING A MEAL

Decide which category and which particular topic you want to explore. Fix your *aim* for the group: 'as a result of this session, I want my group to be aware of ...know ...understand ...'. Then select the main dish which best focusses on your chosen subject and promotes your determined aim.

Choose a starter, and a finisher – if you wish – to complement the main dish and to provide a variety of approach and experience. You may sometimes find you want to choose dishes from different sections to complete your meal. Assemble your ingredients and equipment.

## PRESENTING A MEAL

*Sample A*
You have a group of teenagers and you have decided to help them understand what 'faith' is, emphasising its basic implication of 'trusting relationships with people and God'.

For the main dish you choose the Trust-exercise (Faith 59) and decide to open the session with a starter (Faith 57). It is a simple 'warming up' exercise, but immediately the members of the group are involved together, contributing from their experience and providing a variety of concepts which can be assessed later.

Now you move on to the main dish. For many it will be an intriguing and important experience: in the follow-up, allow everyone to register and share what they have discovered about themselves and each other, particularly their levels of trust and trustworthiness.

At this point you can refer to the starter and compare the original words with those produced by the experience, to highlight your main point.

These two dishes will take about forty-five minutes and should be a satisfying session. But you can add a third dish (Faith 62) to complete the meal with material that is both illustrative and devotional, presenting Jesus as the focus of trust, and faith-trust as a basic religious experience.

*Equipment needed*: Paper and pencils, newsprint and felt tips, blindfolds, New Testaments.

*Sample B*
A group of young candidates (aged twelve and under) has not had many meetings. You have spent time helping members recognise the importance of each individual and form a group in which all feel they have a part. You want now to think together about the Christian community to which they belong, its nature and purpose and its meaning for each of them.

Fellowship 17 would make a good starter, earthing discussion in members' experience of other communities. It should not go on too long as the main dish for the session is Fellowship 22, which again starts with practical experience but moves on to discuss what the Church is, and is for. The leader's main part in the discussion is to draw out the members' ideas and help to express them. The Bible passages should lead to more discussion rather than finishing it with final answers. The written list which emerges from this might be polished for display in church, or it might be better to leave it rough and plan visits from other members of the congregation (Fellowship 23) to help improve it still more.

The meeting could finish with a time of silence (Man and God 42), sharing an idea which has been important in the discussion.

*Equipment needed*: Paper and pencils, newsprint and felt tips, New Testaments.

# 4 DISHES TO SERVE
— *for your confirmation group*

Recipes for dishes are given in the seven sections described in the previous chapter:
> MYSELF
> FELLOWSHIP
> JESUS
> MAN AND GOD
> FAITH
> SACRAMENTS
> DISCIPLESHIP

A list at the start of each section shows which dishes are suggested as starters, main course, or finishers.

Different dishes (in this as in any other cook book) will suit different ages. It is not, however, possible to make hard and fast distinctions about this: 'Ice-cream for the children and stilton for the adults' is a ruling which will seldom go unquestioned. In the same way some groups of quite young members are ready for a depth and range of thought which would leave their parents floundering. So, although suitability for particular groups is sometimes mentioned, selection depends on the leaders' knowledge of their own members.

A book of this kind cannot pretend to cover the whole ground of confirmation training, and different people will, no doubt, identify gaps in different places. The emphasis here is mainly on the ideas which can best be explored by a group through projects, exercises and discussion: leaders will have their own ideas about additional information which is also necessary. In the same way many of the discussions are left 'open-ended' and the conclusions reached will depend on the group and the leader.

The best part of a cook book is often the clippings and handwritten recipes which collect inside the back covers. It is hoped that in this book too a similar collection will be formed of dishes invented, discovered, or borrowed from other sources, which leaders have tried with their group and found satisfying.

# MYSELF

| | |
|---|---|
| *Starters:* | *1, 2, 3, 4, 5, 13* |
| *Main course:* | *4, 5, 6, 7, 8, 9, 10, 11, 12* |
| *Finishers:* | *4, 5, 13* |

1. **My gifts**
   Each person writes down one thing they themselves are good at and one thing each member of the group is good at.
   As each presents their list, the leader writes up the attributes of each person under their name.
   The group compares and discusses the contributions, the resulting portraits and the differences/distortions which are noticed.

2. **My image**
   Each person lists the nouns applicable to him/her self (e.g. brother, daughter, boss, pupil, pianist, footballer. . ), then chooses the word he/she likes to be identified by a. most b. least.
   Explain and discuss in pairs and/or as a group.

3. **My state**
   The leader reminds and suggests to the group what each has brought to the meeting: self, thoughts, memories, expectations, anxieties.
   In silence, or with a background of quiet music, the group members reflect on 'me now', for three or four minutes.
   Each person is invited to say, briefly, what they were most aware of in themselves – and, perhaps, in the others.

4. **My symbol**
   Each person brings to the meeting (after notice by the leader at the previous session) some object important to them, chosen to represent 'myself' (e.g. a badge, a book, a football, a ring . . . ).
   In turn, these objects are shown and explained to the group. Group-members can discuss how far the objects do represent the person.

5. **What I value**
   Each person decides what *five* things they would rescue from their burning house – and why?
   Share and discuss as a group.

6. **Who I value**
   Each person decides which five people they would be happy to share life with on a desert island. These can be real or fantasy people, as the leader chooses.
   Share and discuss as a group.

7. **Self-description**
   Each person writes a description of him/herself under agreed headings (e.g. name, address, rest of family, colour of hair, eyes, complexion, school, work, clubs, interests, personality, good and bad points. . . )
   In turn share this with the group. Discuss and compare, as a group, what is easy/difficult in describing oneself. Why?
   *Variation:* When the descriptions have been written, the leader collects the papers and reads items from each (except the name!)

8. **Self-portrait**
   Each person draws a symbolic picture or diagram to represent him/herself in relation to the things and people and forces (e.g. concerns, desires, pressures) which are important and crucial in their life.
   Share this with another person and/or the group.
   *Variation:* Each person does this in terms of a road-map of their life so far, from birth to the present. Show the good and the difficult bits, blocks, detours, and present direction.

9. **Painting**
   Everyone is provided with brushes, paint and paper; a record of 'atmospheric' music (Stravinsky's 'Rite of Spring' suits well) is played and everyone is encouraged to paint in response to their feelings.
   Afterwards, present, explain (if necessary) and discuss the paintings.

10. **Hopes and dreams**
    Each person reflects on (and writes down if the leader wishes) their own hopes and dreams for the future. They might be helped by listening to a record on the theme e.g. Paul Simon's 'Flowers never bend with the Rainfall'. Share your hopes and dreams with the group and discuss their value: as an encouragement, as a goal, as an escape. (The leader could quote Browning's lines: 'A man's reach should exceed his grasp or what's a heaven for?')
    What ambitions and dreams have been achieved? How will pre-

sent ones be realised or thwarted? What about God's vision for you?
(More suitable for older groups)

11. **Male and female**
    The leader displays materials (adverts, pictures etc.) which emphasise masculine/feminine differences (rightly or wrongly). After initial comment and discussion each person lists the features of his life which are affected or determined by his gender (e.g. choice of work, interests, school subjects, ambitions, attitudes). As a group note any major differences. Discuss and determine which are biological or cultural, appropriate or false.
    If the leader feels competent continue with related subjects e.g. male/female balance in individuals, women's lib, etc.
    (More suitable for older groups)

12. **My history**
    Each person lists his/her interests, hobbies, work, assumptions, beliefs; then decides how and why he/she has come to do these things, determining the origin of each one (own talent, influence of friends and parents and culture, opportunity). Share these and discuss as a group. Together, prepare and present an act of thanksgiving for the influences which have helped make you what you are.

13. **Me**
    Each person writes his 'complete address' i.e. name, house number or name, street, town, county, country, continent, planet, planetary system, galaxy, universe. Now think it backwards in terms of God's creation and concern for people, as someone says 'the universe . . . our galaxy . . . the solar system . . . with about 5 seconds gap between each and ending with place of meeting . . . this group . . . me'.
    (More suitable for younger groups)

# FELLOWSHIP

| | |
|---|---|
| Starters: | 14, 15, 16, 17 |
| Main course: | 15, 17, 18, 19, 20, 21, 22, 23, 24, 25, 26, 27, 28 |
| Finishers: | 16, 25, 29, 30 |

14. **Introductions**
    Each collect the signatures and addresses of all the other members of the group.

15. **Sharing**
    In pairs share space on a piece of paper. Each member has one felt tip pen or a crayon with which to write, draw or doodle on the shared piece of paper. Do this in silence, but talk about it afterwards and then share any discoveries made about sharing with the whole group.

16. **The confirmation group**
    Consider the group and the reasons why members are there. The reasons may be complex, so discussion in pairs first may be useful. Most groups have rules of some sort, either formally agreed or unspoken but accepted. Decide together whether this group needs any 'rules', e.g. are there standards about attendance at meetings, preparation for meetings, attendance at church, which members agree to keep.
    (More suitable for younger groups).

17. **Groups to which we belong**
    On a large sheet of paper draw circles to represent all the groups to which individuals present belong (families, clubs, societies, choir, schools, etc.) and let all sign their names in those of which they are members. Discuss the benefits and responsibilities of membership.

18. **Families and other groups**
    We each have different roles in our own families (brother/son, daughter/aunt/mother/wife/grand-daughter) and the roles affect our relationships. After a discussion of family relationships, consider together the other 'families' to which each member belongs (school, church, club, firm). Are there similar differences of role in each situation? How do the relationships differ? What is our personal role in each group, and how free are we to determine it ourselves?

19. **The organised Church**
    Construct together (with felt tip pens on a large sheet of paper) a diagram of the organisation of the Church in the Diocese. Include parishes, deaneries, archdeaconries, with their councils, synods, and lay and ordained people. Invite people from PCC and Deanery Synod to come and tell the group what they do. Think of questions to ask them beforehand.

20. **Same, similar or different roles**
    Interview a number of both clergy and laity, asking how each see their role in the work of the Church, and how they relate to each other. On the basis of their answers draw up a chart showing their different areas of responsibility.
    How, if at all, do you think this pattern will/could/should change?

21. **The body**
    Read 1 Corinthians 12. 12–27. Then let the group list parts of the human body and try to identify the part represented by each member. E.g. who are the heart, the hands or the eyes of the group?
    (More suitable for older groups).

22. **What's it for?**
    Make a large list of the group's experience of the Church so far, e.g. such words as Sunday, the building, Sunday School, baptism, weddings, services, outings, fetes, funerals, the vicar, the congregation . . . By discussing this try to work out what the Church is, and is for. It may help to read Acts 2. 42–47, Romans 12.4–8 and 1 Peter 2.4–5. See if you can then improve the list together. What do the group see as their part in it all.

23. **The local Church**
    The best way to learn about the local Church community is to meet it. So draw in the help of local members of the Church in many ways. Use their houses as meeting places for the group; divide into smaller groups with special relationship to two or three Church members; use special skills such as music, art, photography which people may have; interview people about their own life and religion and about their part and function in the local church (churchwarden, organist, worshipper, teamaker, vicar, etc).

24. **Being together**
    It is better to experience fellowship than to talk about it, so let the group go out to do something together. This might be going

to a special place or event, or a day out or walk, or work which can be shared. Relationships in this setting are different. Other members of the parish might join (but not swamp) the group.

25. **A fellowship meal**
   At an emotionally appropriate moment, e.g. during or on return from an expedition, have a meal together. It may be possible to find an opportunity to compare (but not equate) the fellowship of the meal with the fellowship of the Eucharist. Alternatively, during the meal a little dry bread and a small mug of water could be shared as a token of unity with the poor people of the world.

26. **Relationships**
   'All love is derived from God, and loving relationships are essential for the development and maintenance of truly human lives'. If this is so, how does the church foster and encourage loving relationships for its members and non-members? Discuss this together in pairs and then share ideas with the whole group. (More suitable for older groups).

27. **Shared concern**
   Plan how the group can find out as much as possible for the next meeting about the work and worship of other denominations in the neighbourhood. This will probably mean allocating different tasks to different members of the group – information to discover, people to interview, places to visit etc. Discuss the group's findings, and consider particular ways in which the different Churches could or should share more together. Do not let this become just idealistic words, but find one small and simple thing which can be done.

28. **Look back in the Church**
   Go as a group to explore the parish church (or if yours is very new a neighbouring one). Use the time, possibly with the help of a local historian, to discover as much as possible about past worshippers. Notice anything which helps you to feel part of a long succession of Christians in the place. Before you leave, join in prayers about past worshippers and your own part today. If this happens in another church, make certain you bring your new insights back to your own place of worship.

29. **How well do we know each other?**
   Spend some time sitting in a circle looking around at each other, thinking how little we really know about other people. Think of

one question you would like to – and feel able to – ask each member of the group. All get up and wander round asking each other the questions. Settle down again for a short silence to pray for each other, ending with 'We are the Body of Christ . . .', the Peace or the Grace.

30. **'We are the body of Christ'**
    Sit together in a circle.
    The leader says the words 'We are the Body of Christ . . .' (from the Holy Communion Service), and this is followed by silence, for awareness of the presence of God and of each other.
    Each in turn then affirms his presence by saying aloud 'I am . . . (Christian name) . . .' round the circle.
    All join hands for the Peace.

# JESUS

| | |
|---|---|
| *Starters:* | *31, 34* |
| *Main course:* | *31, 32, 33, 34, 35, 36, 37, 38, 39, 40, 41* |
| *Finishers:* | *41* |

## 31. People Seek Jesus
a) In pairs, each with a New Testament, take one or two of these passages to read privately:
Mark 1. 40–43; Mark 4. 35–41; Mark 5. 21–24, 35–43; Mark 5. 25–34; Mark 7. 31–37; Luke 7. 36–50; Luke 19. 1–10; Luke 23. 39–43

b) Each pair then tells the group about the incident they have considered, and particularly Who trusted Jesus? What he or she wanted? How Jesus responded?

## 32. Jesus' disciples
Make up and act (perhaps words only, on tape) conversations about Jesus between his followers, e.g. when they first met him, when he first said 'Follow me', when they were tired and hungry, when people turned against him, on Good Friday, on Easter Day, two months later.
This will need preparation – a concordance, information and references.

## 33. Jesus' ministry
Read these passages (each person deals with one only)
Mark 2. 13–17; Mark 3. 1–6; Luke 19. 1–10; Luke 7. 36–50; Luke 13.10–17

*Consider:* What kind of people did Jesus seek out and associate with?
Why did 'normal' people object?
What point was Jesus making?
Share your thoughts with the whole group.
Who are equivalent people nowadays? In what ways can we express Jesus' attitude to them? Show this in a collage.

## 34. The attraction of Jesus
What attracts you to Jesus? Jot down individual ideas and then in small groups draw up a list of key words. These could form the basis of a collage, prayer or poem.

35. **Jesus cares for us**
    Think about the problems which Jesus faced in his time: sickness, poverty, political strife. . . . Are they different from ours today? How did he handle them? How do we follow his example?
    (More suitable for older groups)

36. **Good news**
    In what ways is Jesus 'good news'? Individually think about this and prepare an answer. Each in turn communicates this answer to the group as a piece of good news.
    As a group, discuss how we can share the good news of Jesus with others. What are the problems and the opportunities.

37. **Parables**
    Jesus used parables. Read some less well known ones, e.g. Matthew 21. 28–32; Matthew 13. 44–46; Luke 12. 16–21, 57–59; try to decide what a parable is. In pairs write a new parable which you could tell to colleagues at work, school, etc., tomorrow. Make sure you, the teller, and they, the hearers, would know what the 'challenge' of your story is.

38. **The questions we ask**
    Divide into pairs and let each pair choose one question to ask about the Gospels (e.g. miracles, historicity. . . .). Discuss and try to answer the questions in the group, making sure beforehand that someone will be present who is able to help find answers.

39. **Jesus in the Creeds**
    The Creeds make theological statements about Jesus. Look carefully at what they actually say about him, decide what they mean, and then consider what they fail to convey of the Jesus you see in the Gospels.
    Try to agree upon one sentence to add to a Creed, to represent the missing element.
    Some groups may find they need to use Faith 61 before attempting this dish.

40. **Jesus' death**
    a) Divide into four groups, each to take a different one of the following passages to help them in considering the question 'Why was Jesus put to death?': Mark 3. 1–6; Mark 8. 34–37; Mark 10. 35–45; John 11. 45–53.
    Share the answers together.

b) Now find out what some of the first Christians understood Jesus' death to mean. Each group takes one of these passages: Acts 3. 12–21; Romans 5. 6–11; Hebrews 9. 11–14, 24–28; 1 John 4. 7–14

After initial consideration of discoveries and problems in the small groups, the whole group discusses each passage in turn.

c) What are the main points you would make in explaining Jesus' death to someone now?

**41. Living Lord**

Look at a recent local or national newspaper. Cut out any articles which suggest the influence of Jesus today in the world. Display and discuss.

Finish with the prayer

'Lord Jesus Christ, alive and at large in the world
help me to follow and find you there today,
in the places where I work,
      meet people,
      spend money,
      make plans.
Take me as a disciple of your Kingdom,
to see through your eyes, and hear the questions you are asking,
to welcome all men with your trust and truth,
and to change the things that contradict God's love,
      by the power of the cross
      and the freedom of your Spirit.

*John Taylor*

# MAN AND GOD

| | |
|---|---|
| *Starters:* | 42, 43 |
| *Main course:* | 43, 44, 45, 46, 47, 48, 49, 50, 51, 52, 53, 54, 55 |
| *Finishers:* | 42, 46, 56 |

**42. Silence**
Keep a period of silence together. Prepare for it by discussing what you will think about (something Jesus said or did, personal needs, the presence of Jesus, support for other members of the group, words from the Baptism or Confirmation service. . .). Sit comfortably and try to have sympathetic lighting. Five minutes will be enough for a first time, but can soon be extended. Talk about it afterwards and recognise the difficulties and distractions which we all share.

**43. All our concerns**
In twos or three discuss 'What do you bother God most about?' and then move on to think what other parts of your life could be referred to him. When the discussion becomes general it might be possible to record its essence by having a large sheet of paper and sticking on it at different angles other pieces of another colour and different sizes (size might denote emphasis) each of which has one word or phrase on it (e.g. friends, mountains, maths, poverty, gifts, presence. . .).

**44. A basic list**
Make a selection together from memory and books of a *few* well known prayers which members feel are essential equipment. This might include the Lord's Prayer, the offertory or the final prayer from Holy Communion, the Confirmation prayer, other less formal prayers such as 'Day by day', and several short arrow prayers. Ask someone to type the chosen selection for each member to have a copy. Are there any you would wish to learn by heart? Think about the place of written words compared with one's own words and thoughts. Discuss realistically the practicalities of praying at home, school, church, and elsewhere.

It should be possible to move this discussion on to consider the difference between saying the correct words at the correct time, and the continuing relationship with God.

45. **The Lord's prayer**
    Read the Lord's prayer together, then split into small groups, giving each a section of the prayer to think about, so that they can answer the following questions.
    a. Why do we say 'Our Father'?
    b. What do we mean by 'Hallowed be your name'?
    c. What is the Kingdom of God?
    d. What is God's will for you today?
    e. Why do we say 'give us today our daily bread'?
    f. What is meant by 'our sins'?
    g. 'Lead us not into temptation' – what does this mean?
    h. How will God show his power to us? (Peter 3. 8 and 13)
    Now illustrate your section of the prayer with mimed gestures, and discuss your ideas with the rest of the group.

46. **Not only in words**
    Let the group hear e.g. Michel Quoist's prayer 'Thank you' from *Prayers of Life*, and then compile their own modern prayer, incorporating ideas which are important to them. When this has been completed split into smaller groups for further work on the same prayer.
    Group 1 could use a cassette recorder to add sound effects, e.g. bird song, sea, traffic, laughter. . . .
    Group 2 can arrange suitable music which can also be used in the background, or as introduction and end.
    Group 3 paint to illustrate the prayer on large sheets of paper.
    Group 4 plan and practise reading the words of the prayer, in solo voices or choral speaking.
    Bring the groups together and use their combined efforts to close the session.

47. **Hear our prayer**
    Look carefully at the words of the Intercessions in the form of the Eucharist used in church. Make a frieze, with drawings and magazine cut-outs, to illustrate the various sections.
    Then prepare prayers for one (or more) section for use in church.

48. **Gloria in Excelsis**
    Hear a recording of the Gloria or of the Sanctus and make a painting or collage in response.
    (Hear it once, look at the words, replay while the painting, etc. is going on).

49. **'I opened my mouth and drew in my breath'** (Psalm 119. 131)
    Spend some time in silence thinking of moments in your life when you have experienced awe and wonder. Do not feel they have to be specially 'religious' occasions.
    Divide into pairs and each try in turn to describe your experience to your partner. Share ideas with the whole group and see how these moments of wonder relate to your understanding of worship. You may find words inadequate for this; would paint or dance be more expressive?

50. **Beyond words**
    Look together at a number of pictures in which artists have tried to represent God. These could be in art books from your local Library; the Librarian could probably help you find suitable ones among Italian old masters, manuscript miniatures, Blake, stained glass and church sculpture.
    How far have the artists succeeded or failed? How might a modern painter (or you) attempt to do this? Are verbal symbols any better than visual ones? See Isaiah 6. 1–4 and Revelation 4. 1–11.
    Make a list together of words and phrases which you feel express something about God. It might be possible for adults and some young people to attempt to make a picture themselves.

51. **What do you know?**
    Divide into two or more small groups for a Bible Quiz of sensible questions, some needing knowledge and some needing thought (not from the usual sort of printed Bible Quiz book). This could be done with quick discussion of answers in each group, then group answers compared and awarded marks; or a group form of Master Mind or University Challenge could be devised. Each group would need a Bible. Questions could include e.g.
    What are the two main divisions of the Bible?
    Find Psalm . . . and say what it is about.
    In what book would you find out about St Paul's travels?
    What is an Epistle? Name one.
    Race to find and read Deateronomy 6.5 and Leviticus 19.18.
    Why did St Luke write his Gospel? (see Luke 1)
    What do you think the Old Testament is about?
    What do you think the New Testament is about?
    (More suitable for younger groups)

52. **Bible reading**
    Agree to use Bible Reading notes (of a suitable kind and grade)

for a week. The following week discuss both the content of the readings and what value reading in this way has had for each member. What other ways of reading the Bible might be more helpful? Decide whether to go on, and repeat the discussion and decision each week that the exercise continues.

Individuals differ, and are helped by different uses of the Bible, and the group needs to recognise this.

### 53. Many versions

Plan to bring to the next meeting different versions of the Bible. Work out beforehand what each person can bring, so that everyone makes a contribution and the range is as wide as possible. Include paraphrases like Alan Dale's *Winding Quest* and *New World* and the children's *Listen!* as well as Hebrew and Greek texts.

Select some key passages and hear how different versions treat them. Discuss preferences. Recognise the scholarship lying behind the variety of versions. Hear, if appropriate, an outline of how the Bible came to us.

See and use simple tools for understanding the Bible such as a concordance, commentary, parallel version, atlas. *The Lion Handbook to the Bible* is an attractive reference book which might be included.

### 54. Different ways

Find someone in the area who is well informed about at least one of the main world faiths (perhaps a member of that faith, a missionary, or an R. E. specialist from a local school). Invite him to meet the group and answer questions, many of which have been planned beforehand. The object should be not only insight into other people's beliefs, but also to see what we might learn from them, e.g. the strong family basis of some; commitment; a whole way of life. . . .

### 55. People we disagree with

Let the group share their experience of people they have met, with whom they disagree. What about people with whose religious beliefs they disagree? What should our attitude be to them?

### 56. A pattern of prayer

Some people use the word 'acts' to remind them of four essential kinds of prayer – adoration, confession, thanksgiving, supplication. Others add preparation and change the mnemonic word to 'pacts'.

Discuss what the different kinds of prayer include and, using one or other word as your pattern, plan a short time of worship for the end of the session.

# FAITH

| | |
|---|---|
| Starters: | 57, 58, 65, 66 |
| Main course: | 59, 60, 61, 62, 63, 64, 67 |
| Finishers: | 58, 62 |

57. **What is faith?**
   In pairs or small groups with pencil and paper, each person jots down his own ideas of faith. From these each group produces a list of interpretations to share and discuss with the whole group.

58. **Test of faith**
   Stand in a circle with one person in the middle. This person pivots on his heels and allows himself to be supported by and passed round by members of the circle. Stand close in at first and move further out as the person gains confidence. Change over. Discuss.

59. **Blind trust exercises**
   Each person has a partner. One of the pair is blindfolded. The seeing partner leads the other anywhere he chooses indoors or outdoors for at least five minutes. The time can be usefully extended if space and circumstances permit. 'Obstacle courses' can be set up with chairs and tables. Blind and sighted then change places. Throughout the exercise no talking takes place: contact can be by hand or just one finger. The leader observes particular incidents and levels of responsibility, trust, care, confidence and their opposites. Feelings are shared.
   *Variation*: as above, but with verbal directions and no physical contact. This involves the extra difficulty of following a voice.

60. **Trusting in God**
   Divide into groups of four. Each group takes and reads one of the following passages: Psalm 121; Romans 8. 31–39; Deuteronomy 7.7–11; Matthew 14. 22–33. The groups then plan how they will illustrate imaginatively these biblical experiences and link them with examples of people and things today which we can trust.
   Each group makes a collage of this and when complete presents it to the rest with an explanation.

61. **The Creed**
   Compare the Profession of Faith in the Confirmation service with the longer statements of the Creed. Talk together about the difficulty of putting our beliefs into words. Let each have a typed

copy of the Creed used in church and spend five minutes looking at it and underlining words or phrases which need explaining. Let the group try to help each other with the meaning of the words, but have someone available to help if necessary.

## 62. My own faith
a. In silence for five minutes each person considers 'Where has Jesus been involved in my life?' (This question could be written on a large sheet of paper and displayed).
b. The leader quotes from the Confirmation service 'I believe and trust in Him'. In what situations have you experienced this?
c. Each person is given a pencil and sheet of paper on which are the words 'I believe and trust in Him; so as a first step I want to. . . .' Each completes the sentence for himself. This need not be shared with anyone else.

## 63. Death
The father of Johnny (your godson or young friend, aged six) has just died. What do you, as a Christian, say to Johnny about this? If Johnny were older would you say anything different?
Divide into small groups to discuss and answer this (possibly with a role play including other characters and other points of view).

## 64. God in action
'I shall try to discern more clearly the activities of God in the world'.
Write down individually and then discuss in small groups What you expect God to be doing; Where you see God working in the world; and How you recognise him.
(More suitable for older groups)

## 65. Trust mimes
Members of the group form pairs to think up and mime faith/trust situations in daily life. The leader starts this with a simple example, e.g. a policeman holding up the traffic for pedestrians to cross the road.
(More suitable for younger groups)

## 66. Whom do we trust?
Name people whom we trust. Why do we trust them? Who trusts us? What about? Why? Do we always feel the same about each other?

**67. Case study**
The leader presents a tragic story, either true or fabricated. Discuss: Why do things like this happen to some people and not to others? What is the purpose of our lives?

# SACRAMENTS

| | |
|---|---|
| *Starters:* | 68, 76, 86 |
| *Main course:* | 69, 70, 71, 72, 73, 74, 75, 77, 78, 80, 82, 84, 85, 87 |
| *Finishers:* | 79, 81, 83 |

68. **Celebration**
    Think of ways we celebrate national, local and family events. See what part feelings, food, music, words, dance, have in the celebrations. Think together about the meanings of the word 'celebration' and then use a dictionary to find more. Make a diary of major festivals in the current year – national, church, local, group and family ones.

69. **Signs, symbols and ceremonies**
    Discuss the use in national, social and religious life of ceremonies and symbols (coats of arms, flags, emblems in trade and commerce; the cross, church buildings, spires and towers; wedding ceremonies, funeral customs). Notice the need to express outwardly and corporately things which are of special importance. Discuss the symbols of the two main sacraments of Baptism and Holy Communion, and what they stand for.
    The exercise could begin with a collection of signs and symbols which are then identified and interpreted.

70. **Symbols of celebration**
    All have copies of the Communion service book used in church. Divide into groups, each to read the service from cover to cover, including rubrics, searching for references to: food and drink; music; group fellowship; speech; special events.
    Notice that all these are ingredients of a celebration and construct a sentence which tells who and what the celebration is about.

71. **Join in celebration**
    As a group make a contribution to a current festival, or to a special service (e.g. a pageant or tableau, a musical or dramatic presentation).

72. **What do you hear?**
    Plan to attend a Eucharist and make careful note of what you *hear*. This will include words and music, hymns, readings, pray-

ers, biddings, silence. How much is corporate and how much individual? To whom are different words addressed? Notice different kinds of words – teaching, thanksgiving, penitence, forgiving. . . . Come together to discuss all that has been heard, and draw conclusions about the main features of the Eucharist.

Notice particularly the division of the service into Learning (the Ministry of the Word) and Doing (the Sacrament).

### 73. What do you see?

Plan to attend a Eucharist and make careful note of what you *see*. This will include light, colour, clothes, beauty, movement. Notice the gathering of the people, the entry of the choir and clergy, movement at the Offertory, Peace, Communion, on departure: are there elements of drama in this? Notice the positions and gestures of hands in all this – hand in hand, offering hands, clasping hands, praying hands, blessing hands, hands breaking, hands giving and receiving, hands sending. . . . Come together to discuss all that has been seen, and draw conclusions about the main features of the Eucharist. Notice particularly in this the essential pattern formed by the actions Took, Blessed, Broke, Gave.

### 74. Questions to discuss

Plan to go (together or separately) regularly to the Eucharist, and to meet to discuss it afterwards. Each take a paper and pencil to the service and write down questions (of all sorts) as they arise.

### 75. Ask the right questions

In finding out about the Eucharist have special seats on at least one occasion near the altar, to see what happens. Invite the priest and some of those who are seen receiving Communion to join in a discussion afterwards and say what it means to them. Visit a neighbouring church and do the same.

### 76. Interplanetary explanations (for acting)

Two visitors from outer space describe to each other and discuss the meaning of actions which they see on earth, e.g. peeling potatoes, knitting, directing traffic, shaking hands, waving, saluting, kissing. . . . The earthly participants in the scene tell them the real meaning.

Would the visitors be able to understand the Communion service? How would we explain? Try to make the pattern of the whole service clear to them.

77. **His people on earth**
    Plan to attend a Eucharist to see how the outside world is mentioned or represented in the service, e.g. in the intercessions, the sermon, the giving of money, the offering of bread and wine, the dismissal. In different groups prepare in your own words (following the service book used in church) an intercession for the world, *or* make a chart showing how the world of work is represented in the money, bread and wine.

78. **Of your own do we give you**
    Plan to attend a Eucharist to see in what way the people are offering themselves at the service (voices to sing, praise, confess, pray, express belief: bodies through movement and posture, kneeling, sitting, standing: ears to give attention. . . . ) Arrange for each member of the group to bring a small article which is personal and important (a diary, ring, watch, pendant . . . ), and have them placed on the altar at the beginning of the service. They are blessed and returned to their owners after the service, to express the thought that something of our true selves is offered, transformed and given back at the Eucharist. This may more appropriately be done at a House Communion or a smaller, informal Eucharist.

79. **A painting or collage**
    Make a composite painting or collage representing the Eucharist. Everyone contributes something to it and signs the finished product. It may be displayed in church or presented at the offertory.

80. **Know the service**
    Learn by heart those parts of the service which are said or sung together.

81. **Offering**
    Construct a simple ceremony for offering resolutions (short term and possible ones). For this let each member write their resolution on a small piece of paper and fold it up. These are collected in a dish, formally offered and then burned to complete the offering. The dish needs to be a fireproof one with some crumpled paper already in it to start the fire. The ceremony might be included in the Eucharist, perhaps an informal one or a House Communion.

    A ceremony of the same type could be used instead for each individual to write down and offer to God something true of himself, in penitence or thanksgiving.

82. **Show the connection**
    Make a collage, painting or diagram which shows the relationship between our family meals, the Last Supper and the Eucharist. It may not prove possible to represent visually all the ideas which come out in discussing and planning this. In that case, words could be added to the picture.

83. **Exploring the meaning**
    Explore at a deeper level some of the symbols of the Christian faith. Sit and think about light and fire: a burning candle is put in the centre of the group as a focus for thought; it is then passed round among the members. They can imagine that they are themselves the symbol, and as they hold it say 'I am seen by others, I give warmth, I am being burned, I cast shadows, etc'. In the same way think about e.g. a glass of water, a rock or stone, an open Bible.

84. **Baptism**
    Plan to attend a Baptism. What symbols are used? What is their meaning? What do the parents and godparents say? What does everybody say? Prepare questions to ask the parents or the priest afterwards.

85. **The Confirmation service**
    Divide into pairs. Each pair has a copy of the Confirmation service, reads it and agrees on two questions to ask about it. After these have been discussed and answered in the whole group (or referred to someone with special knowledge to answer) there may still be time for more questions.

86. **Sacramentum**
    Tell about the contract made by the Roman soldier – his military oath (*sacramentum*) in return for which he received his daily rations.
    How does this relate to
    a. the Baptism service – find the place?
    b. the Confirmation service – what corresponds to the oath and what to the rations?

87. **Other sacraments**
    Look carefully in a service book at one other sacramental service (besides Baptism, Confirmation, or the Eucharist). Identify and talk about the symbolic acts involved.

## DISCIPLESHIP

| | |
|---|---|
| Starters: | 90, 91, 92 |
| Main course: | 88, 89, 90, 91, 92, 93, 94, 95, 96, 97, 98, 99 |
| Finishers: | 100 |

88. **The Christian Profession**
    Look together at the profession of faith made in the Baptism and Confirmation services. Plan together how this might be represented visually. Divide into smaller groups to do the work. The simplest form for this to take would be a frieze with magazine cut-outs and felt pens, but more ambitious groups might have other ideas. Find a suitable moment to display the finished work to the congregation and to answer their questions on its meaning.

89. **Something to do**
    Think of a person or people to do something about – and do it, as an act of service and witness.

90. **Keeping and sharing**
    Play Monopoly, or another game of private gain. Discuss keeping things for yourself or sharing in real life. What could one share with whom?

91. **What's going on?**
    Find out from appropriate interviews and/or notice-boards what the local Church(es) is (are) doing for other people locally, or at a distance.

92. **Cost of discipleship**
    Investigate a modern example of a person committed to Jesus. Use a filmstrip, film or cassette of a modern person such as Gladys Aylward, Captain Scott or Albert Schweitzer (your diocesan Training and Education advisers will know what is available); or invite a live person for interview (who should *not* stay for the discussion). Discuss what you have seen and heard. What is involved in discipleship? How does Jesus come into it?

93. **Nationwide**
    With current newspapers, serious magazines, any TV documentary, investigate the national scene. What is good, and what is unsatisfactory in our national affairs. How, as Christians, can you differentiate? Go on to discuss what goals for our fellow-

countrymen we should be pursuing as Christians. Try putting them in order of priority. (More suitable for older groups).

## 94. World-wide
Gather materials (books, pamphlets, film-strips, photographs) which will help the group become aware of the rich/poor divisions of the world (Oxfam, Christian Aid, etc., are obvious source of materials), the historical and present facts, and future projections. Decide whether this is a problem for Christians, and why? What long-term aims should we have? Finally, the group must choose, and set about, a practical task to help people in the 'Third World'.

## 95. One Plus?
Marriage and family, monasteries, communes and aloneness have provided the setting for Christians' home-life. Investigate these institutions by visiting a local monastery or convent or commune; by inviting a member of one for interview; by talking to married couples. Discuss the advantages and disadvantages of each. How did/will members of the group choose their life-style?

What particular qualities and attitudes would you expect Christians to bring into their 'family' relationships?

## 96. Work
The directors of a light engineering firm, employing fifty people in a small town, are considering the purchase of computers and machinery to automate (and reduce the costs of) more of the production processes. (You can invent a name for the firm and choose its product.)

Fifteen people, ten of them women, would become redundant.

Outline the arguments a (catholic) manager and a (methodist) shop-steward could thoughtfully use for and against the proposal and its ramifications.

## 97. Money
The group, with the leader writing down, brainstorms, a list of items (under fairly general headings) on which people spend money. Each member of the group then lists the items according to his priorities, as necessities, luxuries, waste.... Share and compare individual lists. Is there a Christian basis for making and responding to these distinctions? What about giving, investing and gambling – are there any points a Christian should be careful about? (see *Enough is enough* by J. V. Taylor)

## 98. Journey of Life
Each person does a collage featuring the choices and goals they

see ahead of them, as well as past and present achievements. Present these to the group and share comment. Let each person try to indicate how their particular life-pattern is motivated by, or expresses, Christian discipleship.

99. **Sex**

Try to outline, from experience, knowledge, reading and other evidence, typical patterns and standards of sexual behaviour in contemporary society.

In discussion consider:

What attitudes and practices are seriously at variance with a Christian outlook? Is the conservative Christian tradition – that the purpose of sex is the procreation of children – more traditional than Christian?

As you discuss, bear in mind Paul's theological statement in I Corinthians 6. 19–20. Summarise your discussion by producing a 'code of sexual behaviour' for an adolescent.

(More suitable for older groups).

100. **Send us out**

We say 'Send us out in the power of your Spirit to live and work to your praise and glory'.

Spend five minutes setting yourself a target for this week.

# 5 OUTLINING A DIET
## – a report from St Agnes'

We reproduce here, for your guidance and stimulus, notes of the parish education group at St Agnes', Goodly Claptrap, in the Underfoot Deanery. They met last July to consider how the Cook Book might be used in their parish. 'They' are the Rector, who was to lead the adult group of confirmation candidates, Joan Haynes, leader of the young people's club, Bob Fisher, organiser of the Junior Church, Stanley Briggs, lay-reader, Kathy Stone, teacher in the middle school, and Marjorie Wood, the secretary, whom we thank for her permission to edit and reproduce the minutes.

*The Rector* began by recalling that in his two previous parishes he had been wholly responsible for confirmation preparation. He had been happy with the course he had found used in his curate days, compiled by a former Bishop of Ouranga-Tuang. It was with some trepidation that he had come to Goodly Claptrap, where confirmation preparation was integrated with the whole Christian education structure, from cradle to grave, almost! It was a surprising novelty to find Joan, Bob and their helpers dealing with most of the confirmation training – but a pleasant one when he realised their gifts of communication with young people, and the value of a comprehensive and responsible parish training for Christian life.

*S.B.* Appreciated J.H. and B.F's hard work and concern; but believed solid theological teaching was vital for Christians. He and the Rector had had theological training, and the Rector especially should once again prepare all candidates.

*K.S.* remarked that following Jesus was not to be confused with understanding Karl Barth; St Mark had managed without a theological degree . . . In any case they were here to consider ways of using the new Cook Book.

Discussion eventually moved on to the timing of the training. The Confirmation service would be in ten months, next Whitsunday. The Rector would convene his adult group fortnightly, though in Lent weekly sessions might be suitable.

*B.F.* wanted to use the book at the usual Sunday sessions, with special projects in the two half term holidays. Mothers would help supervise them.

*J.H.* had booked a long week-end in the Easter holiday at New Somesbridge Conference House for her group, which would be meeting one evening a week during term time.

*S.B.* recommended a silent retreat for the week-end. Archdeacon Halfright might be available.

*J.H.* explained that her teenagers would find that too daunting a prospect. But they would be exploring the many varieties of prayer, and a silence for a period of hours could be valuable in such a place.

*The Rector* wondered whether the adult group might join the young people on the Saturday or Sunday afternoons.

*M.W.* agreed it was an excellent idea. The interviewing kind of dishes could be used. It was a chance to share different experiences and outlooks and bridge the age gap.

*S.B.* asserted that the truth of the gospel was unchanging, and that discussion simply compromised it.

Uncompromising discussion on this, and unrelated points, ensued, until the Rector managed to turn the group's attention to planning a programme for the three sets of possible candidates. Each leader would already have his or her ideas, and he would welcome the cross-fertilising of their suggestions.

*B.F.* thought that not all sections of the Cook Book were equally suitable for his younger age group. Discipleship dishes were adult in tone: perhaps necessarily so. His children might cover this aspect of the diet by doing practical tasks among the village community. Much of 'Man and God' – apart from the Prayer dishes – had material and implications in advance of his children's experience. He planned to begin by combining or alternating 'Myself' and 'Fellowship' dishes; to move on to some simpler 'Jesus' dishes, 'Faith' and 'Sacraments'. The half term projects could focus on the Church in the community, and some topics in 'Man and God'. He would be using many visual aids – films and soundstrips.

*J.H.* believed the Church's business was to be involved in awakening and sharing life. She would use discipleship dishes frequently – every two or three weeks: Christians should be known by their caring attitudes and practice. The major work on 'Man and God' would be done at New Somesbridge, but prayer – varied and imaginative – would feature in most sessions. She would use, in turn, a dish from the remaining sections: 'Myself', 'Jesus', 'Fellowship', 'Faith', and

'Sacraments' – then return to another dish in the same series. An R.E. teacher friend had agreed to help with 'Jesus' and biblical and religious aspects of 'Man and God'.

*The Rector,* having heard this with interest, thought he might devote two or even three consecutive sessions to dishes from one topic, depending on his group's interest and involvement. He considered 'Man and God' a good starting place, to be followed by 'Faith', 'Jesus', 'Myself', 'Discipleship', 'Fellowship' and 'Sacraments'. He hoped confirmed adults might attend as a refresher-course; it would be valuable for Briggs to share the group's studies.

*K.S.* wondered how other parishioners could be helped to see and do something about their responsibility for all the people being confirmed. Consideration of this was deferred.

The education group agreed to meet again in early October to review progress after using the book for a month – and, indeed all thought it would be essential to meet regularly after that for support and exchange of ideas.